All Pigs on Deck

Christopher Columbus's Second Marvelous Voyage

By Laura Fischetto

Illustrated by Letizia Galli

Delacorte Press / New York

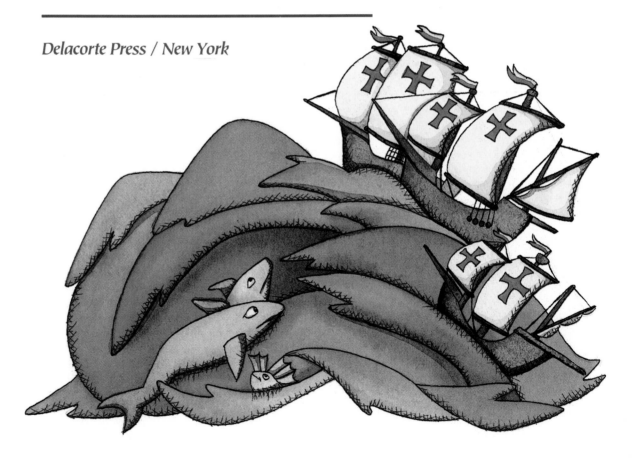

Published by
Delacorte Press
Bantam Doubleday Dell Publishing Group, Inc.
666 Fifth Avenue
New York, New York 10103
Text copyright © 1991 by Laura Fischetto
Illustrations Copyright © 1991 by Letizia Galli

Library of Congress Cataloging in Publication Data

Fischetto, Laura.
All Pigs on Deck: Christopher Columbus's second marvelous voyage / by Laura Fischetto;
illustrated by Letizia Galli.
p.   cm.
Summary: Relates the events of Columbus's second voyage, focusing
on the arrival of pigs in the New World.
ISBN 0-385-30439-0.
1. Columbus, Christopher—Journeys—Juvenile literature.
2. America—Discovery and exploration—Spanish—Juvenile literature.
3. Explorers—America—Biography—Juvenile literature.
4. Explorers—Spain—Biography—Juvenile literature.   [1. Columbus, Christopher.
2. Explorers.   3. America—Discovery and exploration—Spanish.   4. Pigs.]
I. Galli, Letizia, ill.   II. Title.
E118.F53 1991
970.01'5—dc20
[B]   [92]   90-48741   CIP   AC

Manufactured in the United States of America

October 1991

10 9 8 7 6 5 4 3 2 1

The text of this book is set in 16 point ITC Tiepolo Bold.
The illustrations are watercolor with lines in India ink.
Typography by Lynn Braswell

Five hundred years ago, the oceans were just as vast as they are now. But ships were small and fragile, so it was difficult to travel far.

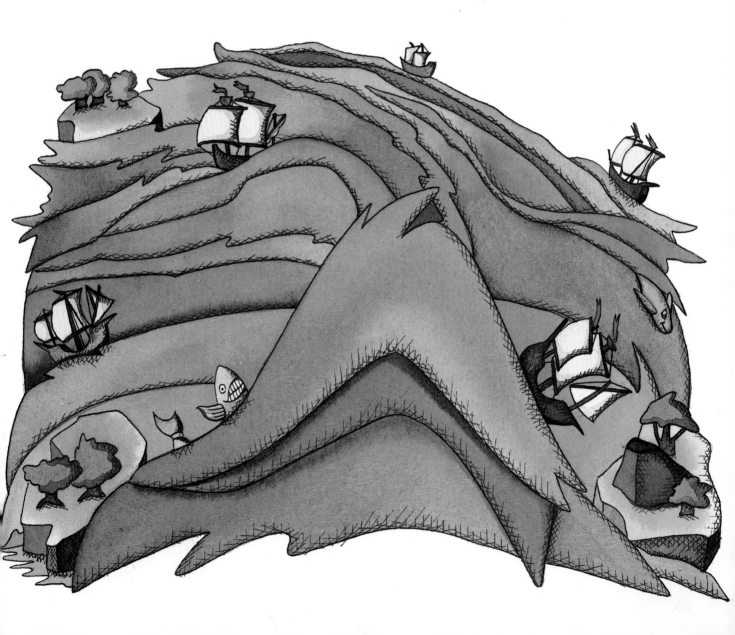

However, a brave man named Christopher Columbus wanted to sail all the way across the Atlantic Ocean. He was so determined that he did.

On the other side of the ocean Columbus discovered a new world. He found many large and small islands filled with strange plants and animals. The islands were very hot and the people who lived on them were friendly. It was very different from the Old World Columbus knew.

During the voyage home, Columbus was
thinking and writing and making plans.
He could not wait to make another voyage.

Many people begged to go on the next voyage, but Columbus knew exactly whom and what he would take along. He wanted seeds to plant and farmers to make them grow, carpenters to build mills to grind grain and painters to paint them.

He wanted tailors to make beautiful clothes for Sundays. He wanted writers to write about all the interesting new things he had discovered, bakers to make cakes, and doctors to cure colds.

Once they had been chosen, all the passengers were in a hurry to leave. They bustled about the ship trying to get the most comfortable seats so they could enjoy the marvelous journey! At the very last minute a little man arrived with all his pigs. Everybody began to grumble, but Columbus refused to put the man and his pigs ashore.

The little man was not a bit concerned.
He plopped himself down right in the
middle of a deck. All the other people
moved away because the man and his pigs
smelled terrible.

By the time Columbus was ready to sail, the pigs were hungry. They started to eat everything they could get their teeth into. Columbus didn't stop them because pigs need to get fat.

Columbus could not keep peace on the ship. For the entire journey, the tailors were mad because the pigs had eaten some of their underwear. The farmers were angry, too, because the pigs napped on top of their sacks of valuable seeds. Columbus did not stop the pigs because, after all, pigs need to sleep.

When a big storm came through, there was a real hullabaloo. The pigs rolled and tumbled all over the ship, and no one could stop them. Not even Christopher Columbus.

Finally, after many days at sea, Columbus
saw land. The passengers packed their bags
and got ready to land in the New World.

The inhabitants of the New World stared in disbelief at all the people. The minute they landed, Columbus set them to work. The carpenters began building, the farmers began planting grain, and the tailors began clothing the island people. The bakers made cakes to celebrate. The island people had never seen such clothes, or mills, or fields of wheat before.

Things did not go as Columbus had expected. The Sunday clothes made the people too warm. The mills sank in the sand. The seeds blew away in the strong wind, and the cakes melted in the hot sun. Some of the travelers began quarreling with the inhabitants of the New World. They could not understand that the New World was different from the Old World, which is exactly why Columbus had returned!

In the meantime, the pigs attracted great interest. The island inhabitants had never seen such nice, fat animals before. The pigs let themselves be stroked without trying to run away, and they were happy to eat almost anything they were fed. The island people wanted to know all about them. The little man happily told them everything he knew about pigs.

So at least one thing Columbus brought from the Old World was suitable for the New. Now, in America today, when we eat juicy sausages and pork chops, barbecued ribs and Virginia hams, we can thank that little man and, of course, Christopher Columbus!

Some Notes on Columbus

Christopher Columbus was born in Genoa, Italy, in 1451. Little is known about his childhood. He is best remembered for his first voyage from Spain to the New World in 1492. On that journey he and members of his expedition became the first documented Europeans to land in the Americas. In all, Columbus made four journeys from Spain to the New World: the first in 1492–1493, a second in 1493–1496, a third in 1498–1500, and a fourth in 1502–1504. The purpose of his second voyage was to start a Spanish colony. With this in mind, he brought doctors, farmers, builders, priests, and others, along with supplies and livestock that included horses, donkeys, cattle, chickens, rabbits, and pigs. The pigs he brought were the first to arrive in the Americas.

Columbus did indeed establish the first European city in the New World on the northern coast of what is today the Dominican Republic. In time, more colonies were established and Columbus became the governor of all of them. However, he ruled far too sternly and persecuted the Native Americans. He was eventually removed from office and returned to Spain. He died in 1506. Today he is remembered as one of the greatest explorers of all time.